T0354756

FROM THE HEART...
AND
OTHER SAFE PLACES

LETTERS AND RECIPES
FROM
ME TO YOU

BY
PAMELA E. JOHNSON

Order this book online at www.trafford.com
or email orders@trafford.com

Most Trafford titles are also available at major online book retailers.

Print information available on the last page.

ISBN: 978-1-5539-5287-9 (sc)

Written by Pamela E. Johnson
Illustrations by Beulah H. Johnson

Trafford rev. 04/22/2020

 www.trafford.com

North America & international
toll-free: 1 888 232 4444 (USA & Canada)
fax: 812 355 4082

In Loving Memory. . .

Dear Gram,

It is now three years later, and I am trying to complete this book. I do not know if I ever told you that I started this book at Christmas a few years ago.

Well I did, and I sent it to a few publishers. I received a positive response from one who told me to add to the pages, and they would consider publishing it. Time passed. You grew ill, and I put the book aside and helped Mom care for you. Frankly, I needed to get past the fear that this indeed might be read by others; my dream might become a reality.

As the days passed I did not think of the book, I focused on work and the hopes of keeping you healthy so you could witness three centuries. Your great big heart gave out at Easter, and we had to let you go on to greater days with our Lord and Savior. You made it to your goal of 100 years on this earth, and you helped us learn to live each day to the fullest.

Well, I let other holidays pass without finishing the book. As the New Year approached and the millennium became a reality, I knew I had to finish what I had started, if for no other reason than because of your example. You taught us to see things through to the end with our chins up. As you always said, "I am not complaining, just explaining". You are dearly missed.

Love and blessings,

Pam

Foreword

My dear friends and soon to be friends, letters are not easy to write. You find yourself putting things on paper that you would never say to a person face-to-face. They are the best way to express your true feelings. As most of you know, I have always enjoyed laying in my bed at night writing to my friends. Many of you have been the recipients of such mail.

Well, the computer age is upon us, and we do not see the use of the pen and ink as much as we should. The personal touch is dwindling. The thought of individuals not writing to each other concerns me. Please read the following correspondence and remember what it is like to share your thoughts with someone who cares. There is a bond between those who write letters and share ideas. It gives us fuel needed to live our complicated lives.

I started with a pen and paper and I will complete my thoughts the same. Please forgive the typed pages (Penny, thanks for your editorial assistance), time and the publisher's concerns led me to the computer. Trust me, the sentiment is from the heart and I will always share my ideas and most intimate thoughts. To prove it, some of our favorite family recipes are included.

Please remember, as you sample the recipes be sure to taste the mixture while you cook. A true sign of a good cook is the ability to taste and adjust the seasonings.

From The Heart...
And Other Safe Places

It is our annual family celebration... Well, if we are going to be truthful (literal) throughout these letters-it is really 1:30 in the morning-after the clean-up. Penny is playing hearts on the computer, and I decided to start sharing my thoughts and our family recipes. As you know or soon will know I have been in the food business for almost twenty years. I have collected and modified recipes forever and have often thought of publishing some of my favorites. But, I have worried about people reading them and saying, "She stole our recipe; oh, I'm going to call my lawyer". I am sorry if that is your issue. I have come to realize that recipes are like letters; they are just a bunch of words until you add your tender touch. Each of the following represents an age old recipe that has been modified as we prepare it year after year.

Mom, Dad, Penny, we have always been a unit. I thank God for my family, extended and all. Your love and generosity have brought me to this point. If the following letters touch other's hearts as I wish, I will continue to bear my load and pay my dues. If the recipes create new menus and family traditions, I can delight in sharing with others.

This book is dedicated to my family with love and blessings!

Pamela

Letters

Recipes

Dear Lord

As we gather around this table, we are united by holding hands to thank you for all of our many blessings. We take this time to thank the hands that prepared the meal and pray for the nourishment of our bodies.

We take a special moment to thank you and pray for the souls of our friends and family who have passed on and rest in your loving care. Family gatherings are so important. They remind us, Lord that we have the power to do your will. In Jesus' name we pray. Amen.

Scratching The Surface

The fashion computer paper that my niece uses to design her gear was in the printer. I mistakenly pulled it to write this letter. It is not a smooth surface so it was not easy guiding the pen, but it reminded me of the bumps and lumps in life that we take along the way. The Lord guides us and leads us. Are we willing to heed and listen, then follow?

This life is so short. We are only scratching the surface. If we do it write (no right) and learn the lessons, the eternal reward will be better than we can ever imagine. Do not let the canvas or the instrument stop you from completing your task. They are just tools along the way. Use them. Learn from them.

Shrimp Cocktail

2 pounds large shrimp (approximately 40), peel and devein
1 heaping tablespoon of Bay Spice

Marinade
2 tablespoons of white wine (or wine vinegar)
1/3 cup of salad oil
1 large garlic clove, peeled and crushed
1 teaspoon finely minced fresh ginger root
salt and white pepper, to taste (just a dash)

Cocktail Sauce
3/4 cup chili sauce
3 tablespoons freshly squeezed lemon juice
2 tablespoons prepared horseradish
2 tablespoons Worcestershire sauce
1/2 teaspoon finely chopped shallot
1/4 cup Absolut Peppar (optional)
dash of hot sauce

Bring a large pot of water with Bay spice to boil. Add the shrimp and poach just until pink and curled, 2 to 3 minutes. Do not over cook!
Drain the shrimp, place on ice and refrigerate.

The marinade is not essential, but I prefer shrimp with a little extra zest. You can skip this stage, prepare the cocktail sauce and serve after chilling. However, if you feel adventuresome, use the marinade, but prepare at least a day ahead.

Stir the marinade ingredients together and pour over the shrimp. Stir to coat well, cover tightly and refrigerate overnight. Stir at least once a day. Remove from marinade and serve with sauce.   Makes 8 servings.

3

Trust Him

You know me well. Your letter came at the right time. I have been having such a hard time making a decision about...life. Should I stay with him? Should I go to graduate school? Should I move back in with the folks to save money? Should I? Should I?

I am too old to be at this crossroad. I have lived a life time and here I am again, redirecting my path. I have the nerve to consider starting all over. I have accomplished more in thirty-five years than some will ever do in eighty. What makes me think I can change in the middle of the stream?

Then I received your note. It is the best advice I can take. What ever is going on in my life, regardless, nevertheless; just trust Him. "What does faith mean?" you asked. It means to believe. God wants us to put our total trust in Him. I will trust Him. I will trust in Christ, alone!

Potato Rolls

1 package of active dry yeast (check expiration date)
1/4 cup warm water
1/2 cup of hot mashed potatoes*
1/4 cup melted butter
1/3 cup sugar
1 teaspoon salt
1 cup milk, scalded
1 egg
4 to 4 & 1/2 cups sifted all purpose flour

Preheat oven to 400 degrees. Soften yeast in warm water (110 degrees if you have a food thermometer). Combine potatoes, butter, sugar, salt and hot milk. Cool to lukewarm.

Add softened yeast and egg. Stir in 2 cups of flour; beat well. Stir in remaining flour (or enough to make a soft dough). Knead on lightly floured surface until smooth and elastic (about 8 minutes).

Place in a lightly greased bowl, turning once to grease surface. Cover; let rise until double (about 1 hour). Press down. Shape into a ball. Cover and let rise 10 minutes. Shape into rolls; place on greased baking sheet. Let rise until almost double in size (about 1 hour). Bake in hot oven (400 degrees) 10 to 12 minutes. Makes 2 dozen.

*Take the time to boil and mash potatoes to insure a home cooked flavor instead of using prepackaged mashed potatoes. When preparing potatoes use a dash of milk and butter to make a soft, smooth mixture.

As The Leaves Fall

The holidays make you appreciate life. They remind you of the simple things. I'll never forget sitting in my window marveling at the gorgeous orange and red leaves. I was peeking through them watching Mommy walk down the street. It was the last day of her radiation treatment. It had gotten to the point that daily I would position myself in the window to make sure I saw Mommy returning home to me.

There is nothing like it. Cancer has taken so many of our loved ones from us. For weeks I had dreams about my breast. I'd wake up and do a self examination; I'd catch myself checking them in the shower. I could not imagine why I was so preoccupied with my health.

Well, weeks later I discovered why. It wasn't me; it was the Lord preparing me for the scariest months in my life. Mommy found a lump and it was malignant. They had to remove it and many, many lymph nodes.

Through prayer and proper care she sailed through the experience. By the Grace of God, I was able to sit on my couch read my favorite floral book (you know that photos of flowers are great for the soul) and watch my Mommy walk down the street. As I watched through the perfect orange and red leaves, she was returning home to me!

Cranberry Sauce*

4 cups cranberries (about 1 & 1/3 12-ounce packages)
2 cups sugar
1 cup chopped dates
1 cup golden or dark raisins (your choice)
1 cup water
1 cup freshly squeezed orange juice
1 tablespoon grated orange peel
1/3 cup Grand Marnier (optional)

Combine all ingredients in a heavy medium saucepan. Stir over medium heat until sugar dissolves. Increase heat, cover and boil until cranberries burst, stirring occasionally, about 10 minutes.

Transfer mixture to a bowl or a jar with a lid. Cover and refrigerate until cold. The mixture will thicken as it cools. This can be made a few days ahead. Keep refrigerated until served.   Makes about 4 cups.

*There will always be someone at dinner who prefers the canned cranberry sauce. Please make sure you have a can or two on hand, chilling in the refrigerator. My personal favorite is Ocean Spray, but, the generics are just as good.

Now I Lay Me Down To Sleep

Girl, I am so tired. I prepared a huge meal for the family. They were in town this weekend. The holidays are wonderful, but let's face it, family can take you places you don't want to be. They can make you go through changes like no others.

As you all know I can only take Dion in small doses. He can be so arrogant. Anyway, this year he brought the tart de jour to dinner. The child was so plastic that I was truly scared for her. She had more silicone in that blouse than the valley and less brain matter than some farm animals. But, she was so nice. Bless her heart, she loves Di Di. (We refer to him as Dion outside of the family--Di Di irritates him). So, you know I use Di Di every chance I get.

Enough about him, my only reason for mentioning him was to get to his date; she shall remain nameless. Because of her I said an extra prayer tonight thanking the Lord. There are so many of us running to the salons for the do of the week. We take precious time to have our hair dyed, fried and laid to the side. For what?

Honey, do not flair up and get mad at me. I am not criticizing your extravagance. Those of you who know me well can attest to my regular salon appointments. My concern is our hiding behind the latest color, the newest sculpture nail or the thousands of dollars in plastic surgery. We are searching for fulfillment that will only come when we open our hearts to a closer relationship with Our Lord and Savior.

Now, I lay me down to sleep. I pray for my sisters.

Potato Salad
-Heavily Garnished-

5 to 6 medium white potatoes
3 hard boiled eggs
1/4 cup chopped scallions (green onion)
1/2 cup chopped celery
1/4 cup chopped red pepper (green if red is not available)
1/2 cup Miracle Whip (mayonnaise if you insist)
1 to 2 tablespoons dijon mustard
1/4 cup sweet pickle relish
1 tablespoon ranch dressing
seasoning salt and pepper to taste

GARNISH
6 to 8 leaves of red and/or green leaf lettuce (washed and dried)
2 medium tomatoes sliced
1 cucumber sliced
1/2 bag of baby carrots (ready to eat)
2 large kosher pickles sliced
1/4 cup favorite vinaigrette
12 medium green olives

Boil potatoes in jackets; cool, peel and cut into small cubes.
Chop eggs and add to potatoes with chopped vegetables. Add Miracle Whip (or mayo), mustard, ranch dressing and relish. Stir thoroughly; season to taste. Chill for at least one hour.

Heap potato salad on the bed of lettuce leaves and garnish leaves with sliced vegetables; drizzle vinaigrette on top of vegetables only! Top potato salad with green olives.   Makes 8 servings.

Don't Touch That

Speaking of family, Uncle Ned (the strange one) invited himself to dinner...some believe in reincarnation and others don't. Well, that is simple enough-or is it? Life can sometimes appear to be a paradox.

I have often wondered if I lived in another time and was abused as a child. I have these intense feelings about child abuse, and I have lived through the pain and suffering of relatives who have been abused by fathers, grandfathers and uncles. The hush, the secrets, the places within themselves where they find safety. It is a terrible, terrible thing to do to a child. You destroy a part of them.

I know this is a sensitive subject for you. But, If I could only speak to all pedophiles, child molesters or the like. I would question if they recognize the hurt they are passing on. Yes, someone may have hurt them as a child, and this sick cycle has continued. How can we convince them to be strong and end this nightmare?

They have to understand that God wants us to love each other as a reflection of His love for us. He would never hurt us. They must stop hurting others. Can we work together to heal the wounds? Stop! Don't touch that. Seek help, seek guidance, seek peace.

String Beans

2 to 3 pounds of string beans (green beans)
1 large onion chopped
1/8 cup sugar
1 tablespoon seasoning salt (or to taste)
1 tablespoon granulated onion or onion powder
1/2 teaspoon freshly ground pepper
1/3 cup white wine
1/4 cup of hot sauce

Remove ends and strings from beans and snap into pieces.
Wash and drain. Place in pot with chopped onion, sugar, salt, granulated onion (or onion powder) and pepper; cover with water. Cover with lid and cook over medium heat for 30 to 45 minutes before adding wine and hot sauce; return to heat and cook until tender. Add extra seasoning to taste.
Makes 8 servings.

Yes, I Have Gay Friends!

Oh! Isn't "gay" such an unnecessary label? People should not dare to compare sins or offer judgment. It is so unnecessary. Believe it or not, we are all the same emotionally and often spiritually. We put our pants on one leg at a time, and if you cut me, cut him, or cut her, we will all bleed.

Jamie called tonight to wish the family well; he is a wonderful man. He has grown into manhood. Boy, when he first set foot in the city, he was loud and flamboyant. I often wondered if I would get a call from the local hospital saying that someone had bashed his face. (Let's recognize, there are many homophobic folk in this world.) But, back to Jamie's evolution. His talents are limitless. He is a designer by trade, and he has such a creative eye. He can make the worst plaid and stripe combination look good. His designs are well worth the money that most spend for the top designer labels.

All of that is history and background information. My main reason for mentioning it is because of his maturity. I was visiting his fair town recently, so I dropped by to check on him. We sat in his living room for hours sipping spiced plum tea and talking about relationships.

He started complaining about his present amour, who is so different and lacks initiative. It is just the same ole' same ole'. So much the same that it reminded me of this man that I have been dating at. I can't say dating since he rarely takes the initiative to call or suggest a date. Yet, he is always willing and excited when I call with suggestions. As Jamie and I agreed, THAT IS BORING!

So, I started the lecture. Opposites attract and someone has to be the aggressor. I know we all like balance, but it should be a give and take. After I gave my speech and tried to shine a reflector on Jamie's negative attitude I saw my reflection also. It made me think long and hard about the situations we find ourselves in and the relationships we should learn from, so we do not keep repeating them. The simple truth is we are all God's creatures, big and small, gay and straight, functional and dysfunctional. Life is one big lesson.

Sweet Potatoes

5 to 6 large sweet potatoes
8 tablespoons butter (1 stick)
1 (22-oz.) can pineapple chunks
1 orange peel (zest only, not the white pith)
1 cup orange juice
1 cup brown sugar
1 & 1/2 tablespoons cornstarch
1 & 1/2 tablespoons cinnamon
1/2 teaspoon nutmeg
1/8 teaspoon ground cloves

Preheat oven to 350 degrees

Boil potatoes until tender, cool and peel. Cut into chunks and set aside.
Melt butter in saucepan, add pineapple with juice, orange juice and spices.
Mix sugar with cornstarch and stir into hot mixture; add the orange peel.
Stir frequently until the mixture thickens. Layer the potatoes in a greased
baking dish. Sprinkle each layer with additional cinnamon and nutmeg;
remove orange peel from sauce and pour over potatoes. Bake uncovered for
45 minutes. This dish can be prepared early and stored overnight.
Makes 8 servings.

Are You Alright?

Daddy's little girl. I am up late (it is almost 3:00 am) writing to you. I am sleeping in a common area since my sister's house is full. Dad gets up to go to "the john" and notices the light. He peeks in and waits a few long minutes to say "Are you alright?"

There is nothing like a Daddy. I love my Mother dearly, but, I grew to love her like this. My Dad is a different story. I have loved him forever. We were running buddies from the time Mom would trust him to care for a toddler. He has been my hero through accomplishments and disappointments. He has worked my nerves more than any man can and ever will but, I love him still.

If you were born an orphan, fatherless after birth or have lost a father at a tender age, look to God, he can be that Daddy. He will be that shoulder on a weary day, that lift when you hit rock bottom, that tissue to wipe the tears of joy. He is a father who cares. There is nothing like a father's concern, someone to ask "Are you alright?" Be still; let Him wait that long minute. If you listen, God will ask.

Macaroni And Cheese

2 cups elbow macaroni
6 tablespoons butter
2 tablespoons flour
1/2 teaspoon seasoning salt
1/4 teaspoon freshly ground pepper
dash of granulated onion
2 cups milk
8 oz. shredded sharp cheese
4 oz. shredded mild cheese

Cook macaroni in boiling salted water until tender, drain and rinse with cold water; set aside. In saucepan, melt 3 T butter, blend in 2 T flour, seasoning salt and pepper. Add milk; cook and stir until thick and bubbling. Add sharp cheese, stir until melted. If you have read this far and don't have the time, purchase a can of Campbell Cheddar Cheese soup and mix with milk and butter.

Mix cheese sauce with macaroni and layer in a greased dish with remaining butter and mild cheese. Sprinkle cheese and granulated onion on top. Bake at 350 degrees for approximately 35 minutes.. Makes 8 servings.

Married Men

I have written this letter far too many times. Lord, I am embarrassed to say that I did not learn the first time and would often date men who were in relationships. You know I am good. I can change them; they will not want to go back. I later realize that I am not the only woman with that pathetic attitude. It is funny; it takes one minute or a new woman to remind us. If we can take him from A to B; the next woman can move him from B to C. The weak man who dates outside of his sacred union will do it with whomever. It is truly not about the woman. It is about the ego; short and sweet.

P.S. Okay, you are different; this is about love and he truly loves you. I have never really convinced myself of that because I was running from a commitment. It was always easier to date someone's man so I did not have to look within and make any decisions about me. What kind of mate would I be?

Just remember, in relationships like this, there is always another chick on the side. At this particular time, the chick is you! Now, is this truly about love?

Roast Turkey
And Cornbread Dressing

8 to 12 lb. turkey
oven roasting bag (optional)
seasoning salt
pepper
granulated onion

Cornbread Dressing
4 cups corn bread crumbs
3 slices toasted bread cubed
1 cup chopped celery
1 cup chopped onion
1/2 cup chopped green pepper
1 teaspoon sage
1 tablespoon poultry seasoning
1 teaspoon seasoning salt
1/2 teaspoon pepper

Rinse the turkey and remove the giblets (reserve for broth); season thoroughly with salt, pepper and onion. Place in pan with oven bag. If not cover loosely with foil; the last 45 minutes, cut band of skin or string between legs and tail; uncover and continue roasting until done. Baste every hour if you do not use the bag. Reserve pan drippings for gravy. Bake at 325 degrees for 4 to 4 & 1/2 hours.

Prepare your favorite cornbread recipe and add the above dry ingredients. Once the bread is done and cooled break into small pieces and add the onion, pepper and celery. Mix with bread cubes and a little of the giblet broth to help bind. Place in a buttered casserole dish and bake for 40 minutes at 350 degrees.   Makes 8 servings

What Now, Lord?

Around the holidays ten years ago I returned home to start my own business. Little did I know it would take so much time and so much emotion. But, thanks be to God, I now can say we are on our way. I finally opened up and let others help me. I gave more of my time as a volunteer and helped those in need. I tithed a tenth, yes 10% of my earnings, with the church to assist in their outreach. I listened to those who have walked the same road, and I shared my trials with those who follow.

I am now at a point in my life where I am searching for new mediums, new ways of expressing my talents. I ask you, what now? When we count only on material gains, we are always searching. We are never full; we constantly want more. When we nourish our souls and understand the Lord's work, we can be filled with an everlasting peace. We can live and enjoy each day as it comes, twenty-four hours at a time.

Giblet Gravy

Giblet Broth
2 tablespoons (1/4 stick butter)
neck and giblets reserved from turkey
discard liver (optional)
1 cup chopped onion
1/2 cup chopped celery
5 cups water
1/2 cup dry white wine (optional)
1/2 teaspoon whole black peppercorns
2 bay leaves
1/2 teaspoon dried thyme

Gravy
Giblet Broth
6 tablespoons (3/4 stick) butter
6 tablespoons all purpose flour
chopped turkey neck meat reserved from giblet broth

For broth: Melt butter in heavy large pot over medium heat. Add neck and giblets, saute until brown (10 minutes). Use a slotted spoon transfer meat to a plate. Add onion and celery to pot. Saute until brown. Add water, wine, neck and giblets to vegetables; bring to a boil. Add all remaining ingredients to pot; partially cover and simmer until tender (1 & 1/2 hour). Transfer meat and chop to reserve for gravy. Strain broth into bowl.

For gravy: strain pan juices from roasting pan and spoon off the fat. Pour juices and Giblet Broth into medium saucepan. Boil until reduced to 3 cups. Melt butter in large saucepan over medium heat. Add flour; cook until golden brown; stirring often. Whisk in reduced broth mixture. Simmer until gravy thickens; stirring occasionally, about 5 minutes. Season to taste with salt and pepper. Add reserved chopped giblets; simmer 5 minutes longer. Transfer to bowl and serve with turkey.

Memories

I was so sorry to hear that your father developed Alzheimer's. We are losing so many of our elderly leaders to that dreaded condition. It is so sad because it robs them of such a delightful experience --remembering.

As I sit here writing to you I remember sitting in your kitchen as a child watching your Dad prepare Sunday supper. I so looked forward to meals at your home because he could fry some chicken, and oh, how I loved his pot roast! Never once did I think how sad it was for you not to have a Mommy cooking. Your Dad was father and mother enough for all of us. He took great pride in making sure you and your siblings enjoyed life--including extending his kindness to your friends.

Because of your Dad, I have fond memories of childhood and weekends at your home. The thoughts are strong enough for us all. As I lay my head down tonight and thank the Lord for my blessings, I will be sure to remember to say a thing or two for your Dad as well. After all, he is a great part of my beautiful memories.

Roast Beef Or Roast Pork

4 to 5 lb inside round (beef)
-or-
4 to 5 lb pork loin

2 large garlic cloves
seasoning salt
freshly ground pepper
meat thermometer

Someone always comes to dinner who can't eat turkey. In this day and age there are often elderly relatives who are bothered with gout (a form of arthritis). If so, they should stay away from turkey and giblets.

You make the call, beef or pork. Then place the meat on aluminum foil and sprinkle with salt and cover with freshly ground pepper. Cut the cloves in quarters and stick into meat in various places. It is easier to insert if you pierce the meat with a knife and insert the cloves. Wrap the meat tightly with the foil and insert the thermometer. Place the meat in a roasting pan and cook very slowly until the thermometer indicates the temperature of choice. Today, health officials suggest all meat be served medium well or well to avoid bacteria. Cook the meat at 200 degrees until done; it will take approximately 5 to 6 hours depending on the size of the roast. The low temperature and long hours is the key to tender meat. Preserve the au jus and serve in a gravy boat for that extra touch.

I Have Never Owned A Dog

My sister owns, well, has a beautiful German Shepherd. He is laying here wishing that I would turn out the light and go to sleep so he can relax.

We never had dogs as children because of allergies, but this is her second Shepherd and the sneezing has been minimal. She always wanted her children to grow up with a dog and to date, they have been blessed with two exceptional animals.

Her children are two of the most wonderful human beings on this earth. Honey, I am not saying this because they are mine. They are wonderful. Her oldest is, well, I will admit he is the apple of my eye. I adore him. He was my 30th birthday gift, and everyday since has been a gift, even when he grates my nerves. Her daughter is another jewel. I love her dearly; she is God's example of how humorous He can be. She is so much like me. The mouth on her takes sassing and determination to another level. The scary thing is she was like that at 8 and I was more like that at 14. She looks like my sister-- as pretty as a picture but, her ways are mine personified. My poor Sissy! She lived with me and was the greatest sister you could ever want. Now, she has to raise me all over again.

God bless them. I have never owned a dog, but by the Grace of God I will never say I have never had children. It takes a village to raise children; and as far as my sister and I are concerned, I have two wonderful children. I am proud to be called "Auntie".

Apple Cobbler

Cobbler Pastry
3 cups flour
1/2 teaspoon cinnamon
1 teaspoon salt
24 tablespoons of well chilled sweet butter
2 eggs
5 tablespoons of cold water
4 teaspoons of freshly squeezed lemon juice

10 to 12 assorted apples (Gala, Granny Smith and Red Delicious)
1 cup white sugar*
1/2 cup brown sugar
1 & 1/2 tablespoons cinnamon
1/2 teaspoon nutmeg
dash of allspice
6 to 8 tablespoons of butter

Combine dry ingredients in large bowl. Cut butter into small pieces and mix into mixture with fork, until it is like coarse meal. Combine eggs, water and lemon juice, drizzle mixture over the flour. Mix with fork until dough blends together. Add more cold water if necessary. Wrap with plastic wrap or wax paper; refrigerate for at least 45 minutes. Roll out on lightly floured board. If making your own pastry is too much effort then purchase two packages of your favorite refrigerator, pastry dough. I prefer the "dough boy's" brand. Mix apples, sugar and spices together and place on bottom layer of dough. Use a long rectangular baking dish. Add butter and cover with top crust, cutting slits for steam to escape. Sprinkle with a little sugar; bake at 375 degrees for one hour and 10 minutes or until golden brown.
Makes 8+ servings.

*substitute sweet 'n low for white sugar (follow measurements on the box); omit brown sugar and make a small pie for your diabetic guests.

Caring Neighbors

Miss Peach is such a precious woman. This afternoon she called to see if we could spare any food from our meal. She was "collecting the garbage" on the block to prepare care packages for the seniors who do not have family.

Often the elderly will not bother to cook for themselves, especially during holidays. Their spouse is no longer living and/or their children are not regular visitors. Instead of taking the time to prepare a meal, they will eat whatever is in the pantry or freezer.

Well, Miss Peach believes it only takes a moment to reach out and share our blessings. This afternoon, she will come by to collect our extra cake. I always prepare more than enough food, and today it will be shared by many. What a blessing. What a peach!.

Pound Cake

1 cup softened butter
2 & 1/2 cups sugar
1/4 cup shortening
5 eggs (room temperature)
1 teaspoon vanilla
3 cups sifted cake flour
1/2 teaspoon baking powder
1 teaspoon grated lemon peel (yellow skin/not white pith)
1 teaspoon lemon juice
1 cup milk

Serve with fresh strawberries (optional)

Cream butter with shortening. Add sugar gradually, creaming until light. Add eggs one at a time, add vanilla and beat until fluffy. Stir dry ingredients together and add to creamed mixture alternating milk, lemon peel and juice; mixing after each addition. Bake in greased and lightly floured tubed cake pan; use bundt if tubed is not available. Bake at 325 degrees* for 1 hour and 15 minutes (watch cooking time, may need 5 to 10 minutes less for bundt pan). Insert toothpick and if dough does not stick, cake is completely done. Cool thoroughly and remove from pan.

*Remember when baking to adjust temperature and cooking time to higher altitudes.

25

God's Grace

Dear Lord, as we gather together, we thank you for waking us up this morning with a sound mind and healthy body. We thank you for our daily bread and the ability to feel the breeze that flows through our window. We know, dear Lord, it is because of your magnificent grace that we can sit here and enjoy this meal.

Thank you for the food we are about to receive. May it nourish and strengthen our bodies for Christ's sake we pray. Amen.

A Slice Of Life

I fell asleep writing. The sun is peaking through the curtain and I can see a thin orange line forming on the wall. Orange, what a wonderful scent, what a wonderful color. There is nothing like freshly squeezed orange juice in the morning. There is nothing like watching the sun rise as it explores the spectrum and shows us every shade of orange there is to see.

Did I ever tell you about the homeless boy that would come by the restaurant in the morning? He would always appear as we were emptying the trash, dumping the peels from the freshly made orange juice. He would refuse breakfast, but I noticed he would scurry to gather as many orange peels as he could carry. After I realized that he only wanted peels, they soon became sections and often entire oranges. He might have been too proud to accept breakfast, but giving him the oranges was my way of saying good morning. I was determined to feed him some way, some how.

It is funny, when I look back at it; he would appear just as the sun met the horizon. It was the prettiest light of day. There was an orange glow over the window that would shine brightly just before the boy came into full view. It was as if orange was the color, the scent that matched his soul.

Today, as we go about our life, our mission, let us take a moment to think about life. What is your color? What is your scent? We take a slice out of life everyday. What is your flavor? What fruit will you bear in this lifetime?

Freshly Squeezed Juice

Grapefruit-Tangerine
2 chilled grapefruits
6 chilled tangerines

Peel the fruit and juice on a hand or electric juicer. Blend. Serve in chilled glasses   Makes 8 servings

Orange-Strawberry
16 chilled juice oranges
12 large chilled strawberries, hulled

Rinse oranges and cut in half; squeeze by hand and remove seeds with a spoon. Puree with strawberries in a blender. Serve at once in chilled glasses.
Makes 8 servings

Smoothie

12 ounces frozen blueberries or hulled strawberries
3 medium peaches, pitted and cubed
2 large bananas, peeled and sliced
1 small mango, peeled and cubed
3/4 cup freshly squeezed orange juice
1/2 cup crushed ice

Peel and cube fruit, place in ziplock bag and freeze. Remove from freezer and blend with juice and ice. Serve at once in chilled glasses.
Makes 8 servings

Deliverance

This place is a buzz. Ruth's water broke in the middle of breakfast. I asked that child not to travel so close to her due date. But, she is so hard headed and a big baby. She hates to miss family gatherings. As upset as we are to postpone breakfast, we are equally excited to get her to the hospital and set eyes on the newest member of our family.

Babies are God's greatest gift. They are warm and cuddly. They smell like fresh air. Their eyes remind us of life's greatest joys. They are the epitome of unconditional love. We have had a lot of babies around here lately. Kelly, the newest dog, is a Cocker Spaniel puppy. You have not seen big eyes until you have seen Kelly. Snowy, the fluffy white kitten, well, I am not fond of cats, but Snowy has to be the sweetest ball of white fur ever. Now, today Ruth's baby. We prayed for a healthy newborn. A blessed birth.

As we stop to say a silent prayer for the perfect delivery, let us remember how blessed we are. God gives us these little creatures; human, canine, feline to help us learn life's lessons. They provide us with the opportunity to not only guide a life but continually nourish and redirect our lives.

God's Grace allows each and every one of us a new birth everyday. Rejoice in the celebration of life. Happy Birthday, one and all.

Coffee

*Start with a clean coffee maker. After each use, clean with soap, hot water and a brush to remove the oils that adhere to the maker. Rinse and dry.
*Always use cold water to make coffee.
*Store coffee in an airtight container in a cool place.
*Measure proper grind of coffee accurately. Allowing two tablespoons of coffee for each cup of water. The proportions may vary with individual taste. After you find what suits you and the coffee maker, measure both water and grounds each time.

Spice It Up

-add a dash of vanilla extract to grounds

-add a dash of ground nutmeg & cinnamon to grounds

-add a dash of cloves or allspice to grounds

Serve It

-stir with a cinnamon stick

-use flavored syrups or raw sugar as sweeteners

-use whipped cream versus half & half

-top with ground cocoa or chocolate chips

Prescription For Living

You tease me about Gram's age constantly, but she got to the ripe old age of 100 by eating properly. We could all take some tips from her. After the birth of her second set of twins, she erased all processed food from her diet. No white flour, no white sugar crossed her lips if she could help it. She refused to eat too many things with preservatives and soaked her fresh fruit before peeling to remove pesticides and auxiliary chemicals.

Vitamins were a way of life. She averaged twenty or so a day. She was sure to get vitamin A, B, C and always E in her system daily. Never did she pop an aspirin, and until the day she died the doctor could not get her to take much to relieve discomfort. For Gram, it was the natural way or no way. She knew most homemade remedies to prove it.

Today, there is so much talk about the importance of water to our diets. Hinkley & Schmitt delivered water to Gram for as long as I can remember. According to her, the stuff that comes out of the faucet is not fit to do your dishes. So, when she ran out of water before her next delivery, we purchased from the store or she boiled and strained the tap water.

Gram truly believed that we are what we eat. She believed that our bodies are our temples. They house the soul, and we have to take great care in preserving the temple. "Our bodies are on loan" she would say. Gram always taught us to take great care of that which is loaned to us... "Treat it better than you would ever treat something of your own. It is a temporary gift."

Fresh Fruit Salad

2 seasonal melons (preferably, cantaloupe & honey dew)
1 pineapple
1 mango
1 pint strawberries*
1 cup red or green seedless grapes
2 bananas
juice of 1/2 lemon
1 tablespoon honey
1 cup coconut (optional)

Peel and remove seeds from melons and mango; peel and core pineapple. Cut fruit into chunks. Rinse and dry strawberries & grapes and slice in half. Peel and slice bananas into chunks and mix with lemon juice and honey. Pour off juice and add bananas to fruit mixture. Mix fruit thoroughly. Preheat oven to 375 degrees. Place coconut on baking sheet and toast until lightly brown (about 5 minutes). Watch coconut carefully do not burn. Cool and sprinkle coconut over fruit mixture.
Makes 8 servings

*If strawberries are out of season and they need a sweet lift, sprinkle with one or two tablespoons of sugar and juice of 1/2 lime. Toss before stirring into salad.

Precious Cargo

Before we could finish preparing breakfast and settle in, the telephone started ringing. It was Jordan's Mom calling to say her granddaughter had been kidnapped. It appears that her son was dropping the oldest child at daycare and left the baby in a running car. A carjacker jumped in and stole the car with the baby in the back. Honey, I will not keep you in suspense; the baby was found unharmed, a few hours later. The thief left the car outside of a police station.

Our prayers were answered; apparently this was just a car thief. He was not a pervert preying on innocent children. It is a sad testament of our society when we can qualify by "just a car thief". But, it is an even sadder realization that in today's busy world parents leave their children in cars to run a "quick" errand. They are too concerned about the time involved to unhook car seats, unload the car, hold hands and bumble in and out of day cares, cleaners and/or the corner store.

We have been entrusted with little human beings. We need to focus on their lives and value their existence. We have to take the time to care. They are precious gifts from God.

34

Pancakes

1 & 1/4 cups all-purpose flour
2 tablespoons granulated sugar
2 teaspoons baking powder
dash of salt
1 beaten egg
1 cup milk
1 & 1/2 tablespoons cooking oil

Stir together flour, sugar, baking powder and 1/4 teaspoon salt. Combine egg, milk and oil; add to flour mixture. Stir until blended but still slightly lumpy. Lightly butter (you may use a cooking spray) a skillet or griddle. Pour about 1/4 cup of batter into hot skillet. Cook until lightly browned on the bottom approximately three to four minutes, when it is ready to turn the batter has tiny air bubbles. Please note, if you are adding fruit, add before turning the pancake. Continue to cook on the other side until brown. Serve or hold in a 200 degree oven for up to 15 minutes. Makes about eight, 4-inch pancakes or twenty-five dollar size.

*Pannacakes" (some toddlers add the "na") are a family favorite. Add an extra touch with a dash of cinnamon or vanilla extract. Enjoy with bananas, strawberries or frozen blueberries. Especially when adding fruit, do not cook with very high heat; they will brown and still be raw in the center.

The Eating Never Stops

Why are you so obsessed with your body? If you write me one more letter about a diet, I am going to scream. Honey, you are fine; everyone is not meant to be a size 8. You look great in your 12 jeans. Are you healthy and eating properly? Are you exercising? That is more of a concern.

I am curious about your eating habits. Are you eating a substantial breakfast? Yes, it is still the most important meal of the day. I have read enough to also believe that lunch should be a larger meal than dinner. It should be full of nutrients because you are eating in the middle of the work day. So, by dinner a lighter meal with salad, poultry or fish and a vegetable should suffice. We should also try to sneak fruit and vegetables into each meal.

Are you drinking at least six glasses of water a day with juices and other beverages? Are you watching your caffeine intake? These are more of my concerns than your fitting into a size 8 jean. Take the clothes off of the tread mill. Unhook your bicycle from the patio fence and exercise. They say that women, especially our age need to exercise more. Please eat healthier, drink lots of water and exercise. Then write to me about how amazed you are to fit into those size 10 jeans. We will compromise with the size.

36

Lighter Breakfast Fare

TRY...

chicken sausage
roast chicken
roast turkey breast
smoked salmon
smoked whitefish
soy burger
turkey bacon
turkey sausage
vegetable patty

PREFER PORK?

canadian bacon
roast tenderloin

Say Cheese!!

If I have told you once, I have told you a thousand times. As long as I have known you, you refuse to smile for photographs. I opened the card after brunch, and there it was another one of your serious pictures. You obviously love taking photos because you send one twice a year. But, can we get you to smile?

You are one of the most loving human beings I know. But, people are scared to approach you because you come across so serious and often "mean". Those who know you realize that it is no more than a defense. You are too concerned about letting the world in; heaven forbid if people saw you for the kind person that you truly are. Those who are trying to get to know you are leery.

Smile, my friend. You have a beautiful face and all of your teeth. On a serious note though, smiling is important; laughter is good for the soul. Our souls need nurturing and fulfillment. There is no better food for the heart and soul than a smile. You are as pretty as a picture, sweetheart. Smile, you are loved.

Frittata

10 eggs
1 cup half & half
1 tablespoon season salt
1/2 tablespoon freshly ground pepper
1/2 tablespoon granulated onion (or onion powder)
dash of nutmeg
1/2 cup chopped scallion
3/4 cup shredded cheddar cheese
1/4 cup shredded parmesan cheese
1 package frozen chopped spinach (optional)

Preheat oven to 350 degrees; grease 2 quart rectangular casserole dish with butter (or cooking spray). Defrost, drain and remove excess water from spinach. Lightly scramble eggs and add seasonings, half & half, onion, cheese and spinach. Pour into casserole. Bake 30 to 40 minutes, eggs will puff while cooking and flatten out once cooled. Shake pan before removing from heat to make sure the center is done.
Makes 8 servings.

I Can Do All Things Through Christ

Dear Lord, thank you for all of your blessings. I thank you for the ability to prepare this meal and trust that it will nourish my body. I count on you Lord and the wonders of your grace. Please continue to guide and protect me Holy Spirit. In Jesus' name I pray. Amen.

Shared Experiences

Yes, as much as I enjoy cooking, I hate to wash dishes. As a child, my ankles would itch the entire time I did dishes. Psychosomatic you say? Probably, but I have a choice now, and the itching has stopped. I can leave a sink full of dishes for a week and continue to empty the pan and pour clean water over them with a dash of bleach. The bleach helps keep the smell down and the critters away.

Why not just wash you ask? Because I do not have to! I think life is about shared experiences. If I cook, you should clean the dishes. If I do laundry, you should clean the bathroom. If I keep the house tidy, you should mop and by all means take out the trash.

But, since I am single and no one presently shares the responsibility, I wait until I can not take the clutter any longer. Then, I wash the dishes. I make the choice.

Club Sandwich

2 slices roast turkey
2 slices roast beef or pork
2 slices tomato
3 slices avocado
2 slices cucumber
Boston or Green/Red Leaf Lettuce (if you insist-Iceberg)
1 slice cheddar and provolone cheese
2 slices wheat bread*
1 slice french or sourdough bread
dijon mustard
Miracle Whip (Mayo, if you must or oil and vinegar)

Spread wheat bread with condiment of choice. Layer on turkey alternating with cheddar. Spread french bread with mustard and place on top with lettuce, avocado, cucumber and tomato. Layer on beef/pork and provolone, place remaining slice of wheat and fasten with toothpick. Serves 1 or 2, if you care to share.

*Thinly slice bread and vegetables for this sandwich. Fruit and nut breads are a nice substitute for the french bread. You may toast bread for variation.

43

Lighten The Load

I guess you say, how dare I sit in this sunny city writing to you about winter! But, you know me well, I have guts enough for the two of us. I received your note and I am sorry that cabin fever has taken over. They say, it is the worst winter in thirty years. Trust me. There is a light at the end of that snowy tunnel.

You are much too hard on yourself. Yes, you should expect to feel down when tired, frustrated and caught in the worst snow storm in years. No, you did not prepare, so you do not have proper savings or income at this point in your life. You have always lived by the seat of your pants and did not expect the snow to keep you from free lancing.

But what disturbs me more is your recent state of mind when things are going well. You appear to be depressed, my friend. You have such a negative view of the world. Why?

Focus on your health, your drop dead gorgeous body, your intellect, your sense of humor, your wisdom and insight. Yes, you have the right to be angry. You have suffered several blows. You have not slept well in months, and Satan is busy directing a fabulous pity party in your honor. Don't let the devil confuse and discourage you.

Please be aware of your needs. You have reached a point in the wilderness where you need emotional and physical rejuvenation. Believe it or not, depression often goes away by itself. Make room for happier times by resting and reading spiritually uplifting words. Recognize the problem, understand it, deal with it and dump the excess baggage. God understands our needs and bears our burdens. He is an ever present help; please make room for His comfort. Trust God; there is a healing for your soul.

Garbage Salad

2 stems scallion diced into small pieces
1 small red or green pepper coarsely chopped
1 apple (Gala or Granny Smith) peeled and coarsely chopped
1 avocado peeled and diced into small pieces
1 jar marinated artichokes, drained and chopped
3 medium plum tomatoes chopped
1 large carrot coarsely grated
1 medium cucumber peeled and chopped
2 boiled eggs chopped (optional)
8 medium green or black olives sliced
1/4 cup dried cranberries (optional)
Mixed Greens: 1/2 head Romaine, 1/2 head Green/Red Leaf & 1 small head Bibb

Rinse, drain and spin lettuce to discard excess water. (If you enjoy salad and do not have a lettuce spinner, get one). Tear into small pieces and alternate lettuce with chopped vegies as you layer into large salad bowl. Mix thoroughly and serve with favorite vinaigrette and ranch dressings.
Makes 8 servings.

Leftovers

I am as guilty as you are. It is a terrible habit, but we suffer from low special esteem. We know in our heart of hearts that we deserve better, but we let men get away with treating us any which-a-way. All that to say, we have a man. But, do we? We are really just sharing the lot. We rent them from "the stable" by offering our time and emotions as payment.

Let us make a pact; a New Year's resolution that we will stick to starting now. This year, we will value our time, energy and personal well-being. We will stay home and read, write letters or just take a candle lit bath before we stoop to date just anybody. We will truly be selective and not have the same bad meal twice.

Turkey Hash

1 tablespoon olive oil
1 medium white onion, coarsely chopped
1 small red & yellow peppers seeded
1 clove garlic minced
1/2 teaspoon crushed sage
1/8 teaspoon crushed red pepper (optional)
1 teaspoon season salt
1 teaspoon freshly ground black pepper
2 pounds roast turkey chopped
2 pounds peeled white potatoes boiled and cubed
1 cup broth (turkey, chicken or vegetable)

Chop or thinly slice onions and peppers. In large skillet, heat oil. Add onion, peppers and garlic. Saute about 2 minutes. Stir in cooked turkey and potatoes, saute about 4 minutes until potatoes are browning. Add 1/2 cup broth and heat 5 minutes. Add additional broth and reduce heat to simmer; cook uncovered about 5 to 7 minutes
Makes 8 servings

A Little Something Extra

What does it take? We are always so worried about our time and the next project that we do not take a moment for ourselves. When was the last time you meditated or relaxed in a hot tub and thought about your blessings? When was the last time you stopped and helped an elderly person across the street with their packages? When was the last time you handed a homeless man, rummaging through the trash, a few dollars? When was? When was?

We have to stop and smell the roses. We have to learn to linger and enjoy the sweet smell of rain. We have to value the short time we have on this earth and glorify in the moment. It has been said so often that it has become a cliche; but life is too short.

Let us throw away the worries and surrender the inhibitions. Let us remember, it is the little things that make a difference. Take time for yourself today and make time for others.

Garlic Bread

1 loaf thinly sliced french or italian bread
1/2 cup butter
3 tablespoons olive oil
2 cloves garlic finely chopped
2 tablespoons crushed basil
1 tablespoon crushed oregano
1 teaspoon granulated onion
2 tablespoons grated parmesan cheese

Place bread on large piece of foil. Melt butter in skillet and add all other ingredients except cheese. Dip each slice of bread into mixture and stack to retain the loaf shape. Sprinkle the cheese on top of the loaf. Wrap tightly with foil and bake at 350 degrees for 15 minutes. Serve warm. Makes 8 servings

Bless Me, Heavenly Father

Now, I lay me down to sleep. I pray the Lord my soul to keep. If I should die before I wake, I pray the Lord my soul to take. God bless Mommy, Daddy and Sissy. Please bless all my friends and all my relatives. I thank you for this day and for the promise of tomorrow. I thank you for the birds that sing. I thank you for the food we eat. I thank you for the clothes we wear. I thank you God for everything. Amen.

A Love Like This

I can not forget my sweetie! I know you hate the holidays since you can rarely enjoy them with your family. I know being on the road is tough, but if you look at the big picture you have been blessed. You have a wonderful career, a job that has brought many rewards.

How many times have I written to you? After looking back on it, I must have been obsessed. My "Basketball Jones"; I truly loved you. Your shy demeanor yet, strong public appeal. I watched you night after night bouncing that ball down the court. You were so strong on and off the court. And let us not forget as cute as a button. I was determined to build a friendship and that we did. Now, here we are fifteen years later still flirting on the telephone, writing letters and suggesting a rendezvous that should not take place.

I sat up night after night writing love letters, making cute gifts, baking chocolate chip cookies --all to suit your fancy. A woman should love like that at least once in her life, even if the relationship does not survive.

I am glad to say that my passion continues, it did not die with the end of our relationship. I have moved on to learn from other unions. But, I still had to take a moment to wish you well and remind you that the flame still flickers.

Chocolate Chip Cookies

2 & 1/4 cups all purpose flour
1 teaspoon baking soda
1/2 teaspoon salt
3/4 cup brown sugar
3/4 cup sugar
1 cup butter (do not soften)
2 teaspoons vanilla extract
2 eggs
1/2 teaspoon nutmeg
dash of cinnamon
1 cup chopped pecans
2 cups (12 oz. package) white chocolate chips

Preheat oven to 325 degrees. In a medium bowl combine all dry ingredients and mix thoroughly. In a large bowl with electric mixer combine sugar and then add butter slowly to break into small chunks; increase speed and cream butter and sugar. Add eggs and vanilla, mix well. Add dry ingredients on a low speed until mixed, then add chocolate chips (semi sweet, if you do not like white) and pecans; mix well. Use a tablespoon to drop dough on ungreased cookie sheet, spacing them 2" apart. Bake for 20 minutes at 325 or until golden. Transfer onto cooling rack immediately. Makes 2+ dozen cookies for the kids at heart.

The Finish Line

What a great feeling it is to complete a task, achieve a goal. Life passes so quickly, and we can never remember all of the wonderful ideas that God places on our mind. We just live hurrying through our accomplishments. We need to remember to keep the eye on the prize. The day we face judgement, recall how we lived and all of life's lessons; will also be the day we receive our key to the kingdom or the shanty.

The greatest prize is God's Grace. It is our salvation, if you know that, no one can take it away. God is faithful. The road to our treasure is paved to allow us to help each other. We should live life in a way that sets a good example for all.

Cocoa

1/3 cup dry cocoa
1/3 cup sugar
1/2 cup water
3 & 1/2 cups milk
1/2 teaspoon vanilla
whole nutmeg

In a saucepan, mix cocoa and sugar; add water and bring to a boil. Stir constantly for 1 minute and stir in milk. Heat to a boiling point (do not boil, milk will form a thin film on top, if boiled). Add vanilla and beat with a whisk or rotary beater just before serving. Sprinkle each cup with a dash of freshly grated nutmeg.   Makes 4 servings

Special Thanks
To My Illustrators

I am quite proud to say that the cover and chapter illustrations were done by my Mommy. She is a talented artist, who has always expressed herself for fun and never profit. This same pride extends to my niece, who drew the hands adjacent to the inside cover. As you can see, at age twelve she is learning and walking in her Grandmother's artistic footsteps. Ooops, I cannot forget Auntie Bert (Mom's twin); she helped design the cover!

This has been a wonderful journey, three generations working to illustrate one book. I was raised with grandparents, great grandparents and at an early age great great grandmothers. I never thought about the aging; we were just all on the same train moving in the same direction.

You never really think about age when you are young and full of energy. But, now that I am 45 with teenagers buzzing around me, I think about the fact that society is getting older and older. I am part of that movement. I am not a kid anymore and I cannot just blow by on pure energy.

We have to bridge the gap in society. We need to be more aware of who we are and how we reach up to the elderly and reach down to the youth. The connection is too important to overlook. There is so much to learn from each other. God planned for each of us to experience the aging process and learn from it.

Regardless of your religious beliefs, we all know the story of Noah being 600 years old when he trusted God and the flood waters came on the earth. You are never too old to learn; you are never too old to share. We flutter around in a world that increasingly offers less to hold on to in every way. Find hope for humanity and reach out to one another, young and old.

One Last Treat...
Peanut Butter Cookies

1/2 cup butter
1/2 cup chunky peanut butter
1/2 cup granulated sugar
1/2 cup brown sugar
1 egg
1/2 teaspoon vanilla
1 & 1/4 cups sifted all purpose flour
3/4 teaspoon baking soda
1/4 teaspoon salt
1/8 teaspoon freshly ground nutmeg
2 cups (12 oz. package) peanut butter chips

Cream butter, peanut butter, sugars, egg and vanilla. Sift together dry ingredients; blend into creamed mixture, adding chips as you blend. Shape in 1 inch balls; roll in additional granulated sugar. Place 2 inches apart on ungreased cookie sheet. Press the top with fork tines. Bake at 375 degrees for 10 to 12 minutes. Cool slightly and remove from pan; place on cooling wrack or wax paper.   Makes 4 dozen

Epilogue

My Dear Family and Friends,

It has been my pleasure knowing each and everyone of you. Your ideas, your thoughtful ways have brought me to this point. I have had some of the same friends since second grade. I made dear friends in college and gained more friends and family along the way. I have lived a wonderful life and look forward to exceptional experiences and relationships.

I have been blessed with a dear family. Can you believe Gram's 100th birthday was on Thanksgiving? Yes, I realize that I have a lot to be thankful for, but what a headline!

As I approach another day I look forward to many years of writing letters and sharing recipes. The art of writing dates back hundreds of years. I trust modern technology will not ruin our desire to correspond. There are blessings in letters written from the heart...and other safe places.

May each day be a holiday.

God's Grace,

Pamela

Onward

Thanks for taking the time to read the letters and hopefully experiment with some of the recipes. I finally finished this book when I realized that it could serve another purpose. My concern about writing is genuine. If we take a moment out of our busy schedules to connect through the written word, everyone will benefit.

There have always been strong advocates for our children to learn to read and write. Over the last few years, there has been a huge campaign to encourage reading for our children as well as adults. Book clubs have sprung up all over the world. We need to continue the campaign and expand it to include writing. Because of that belief, I am encouraging a nationwide effort to connect our youth with adults. I truly hope that seniors will become involved, they have a wealth of experience to share. Hopefully, this will inspire a long relationship of writing to someone who cares.

Consider contacting churches and social service agencies to generate a list of youth who would like and/or desperately need a pen pal. You can write to them at the agency to protect the privacy of the minor's address. If you too have concerns about privacy you may use your office or P.O. Box as a mailing address.

Please take a moment to think of how special it would be for someone to receive mail from a person who takes the time to care. Start today to find youngsters who need to hear from you on a regular basis; a youth who needs to practice writing as well as reading. Make the effort, and the blessings will flow.

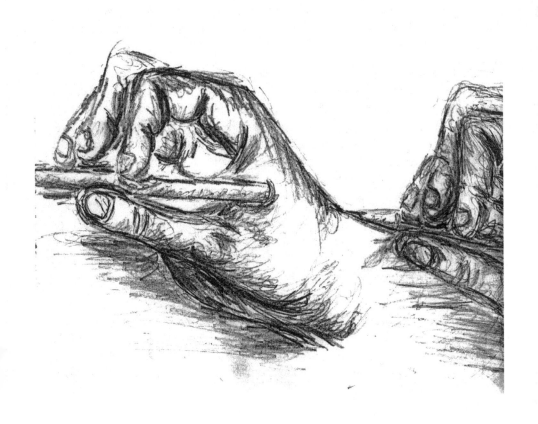

Notes

Printed in the United States
by Bookmasters

Printed in the United States
By Bookmasters